By John Hugh Roberts
Illuminations by Leo Del Pasqua
Produced by Dale Bertrand

THE THREE MERMAIDS

Book Credits:

Original manuscripts written by John H Roberts

Introduction, book design & production Dale Bertrand

Illuminations/borders Leo Del Pasqua

Book Design, Intro & Fellow Adventurer Della Burford

Photography Della & Dale

Azatlan Publishing
Three Mermaids

ISBN 978-0-9878302-7-2

Roberts Heritage Foundation
http://www.azatlan.com

Contact: Dale   azatlan@yahoo.com

Distribution: Signed copies at www.azatlan.com
regular copies at www.amazon.com

'The Three Mermaids' was
written at the turn of the century
by John Hugh Roberts
an Early Canadian writer from Wales
The Illuminations for the series were
commissioned by Dale Bertand
and completed over a three year
period in the early 1980's by
Leo Del Pasqua.

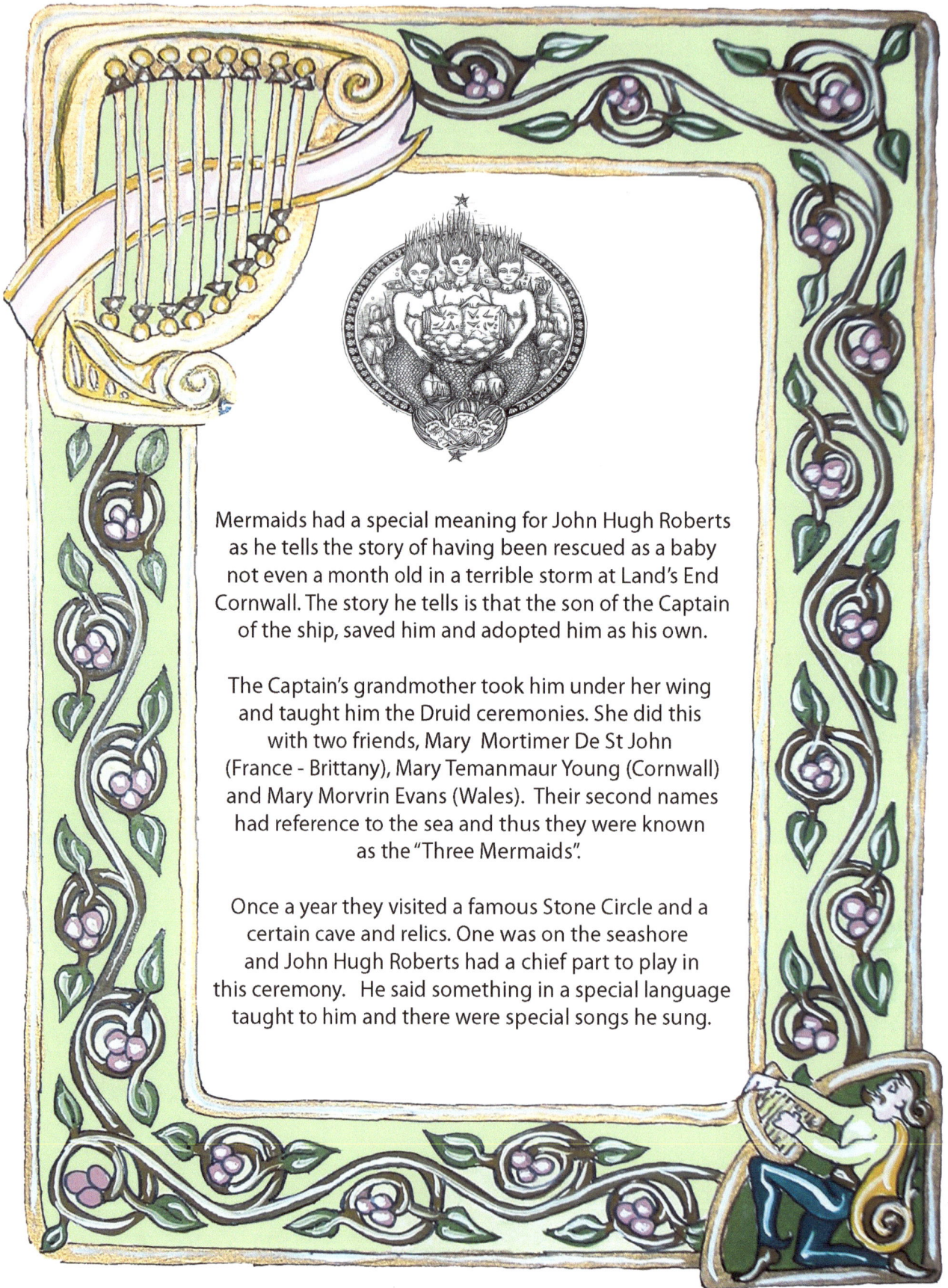

Mermaids had a special meaning for John Hugh Roberts
as he tells the story of having been rescued as a baby
not even a month old in a terrible storm at Land's End
Cornwall. The story he tells is that the son of the Captain
of the ship, saved him and adopted him as his own.

The Captain's grandmother took him under her wing
and taught him the Druid ceremonies. She did this
with two friends, Mary Mortimer De St John
(France - Brittany), Mary Temanmaur Young (Cornwall)
and Mary Morvrin Evans (Wales). Their second names
had reference to the sea and thus they were known
as the "Three Mermaids".

Once a year they visited a famous Stone Circle and a
certain cave and relics. One was on the seashore
and John Hugh Roberts had a chief part to play in
this ceremony. He said something in a special language
taught to him and there were special songs he sung.

John Hugh Roberts discovered the Stone Book
with the Mermaids help and writes it was not
written by one person but by hundreds of people.
He copied some parts of the 'Book in Stones' that is
shared in the 'Stone Book of Knowledge.'

He claims that at "Sarn Badric" on Cardigan Bay,
where the Land of Mythical Teman is purported
to be, that at a certain time of the year questions
are answered from "below the sea".

This may have been another reason for the
naming of these three woman mermaids as some
of the ceremonies he writes about takes place near-by.

There is also an old legend of a Mermaid in a town
called Zennor in Cornwall that goes back to 1600
with a carving in the local seaside church showing
this mysterious mermaid.
Again this village is near one of the stone circles and
the cave where ceremonies that the Three Mermaids
participated in.

There are many different stories of mermaids.
For now lets enjoy the "Three Mermaids".

The Three Mermaids.

in the year 1800. at a gay Ladys school in the west of England
three gay Ladys heretofore Strangers. to each others, became fast-
friends, their names in full were, Mary Mortimer de St John,
Mary Temanmaur gay. & Mary Morwin Evans. the first was
a Native of the west of France (Britagy) the 2nd of the west of England
(Cornwal) and the third from the west Coast of Wales. the curious
Part about them is that their names are nearly of the same literal -
meaning. John, gay, & Evans. all mean young. and the second name
Mortimer - (Sea of the house of Mer — Mercury) Temanmaur (môr) House of
man — Place, of the Sea. Morwin (Sea of the Hill — Maunt) and became
of this refference to the Sea. dauntless, they received the name of Mermaids.
when I was a boy the three resided in Cornwal. and ance evry year —
they (with others) visited a famous Stone Circle, and a certain Cave & Relics.
observing some Ceremonies, the object and nature of which at
that time was unknown to me. particularly the one on the Seashore. in which I allways appeard as having the chief Part to Play.
I was taught to say a number of verses in a Language unknown to me
then, but which I have lately discovered what it was. or partialy so at least.
M. M. E. Maried one Captain Roberts. a Native of Cornwal. the
the other two as far as I know were never maried. the eldest son
of Captn R. also became a Captain & part owner of the Ship —
I was taught, and belived. that he was my Father. but recently I
have discovered. that he had Saved me when a baby not a Manth
old. from the Shipwreck of his Ship. on bard of which I had been
since the 2nd or 3rd day after my birth — and he had adapted me as his Son
my own Parents having been lost in the Shipwreck. whoever they were.
If I had only even suspected. these particulars. when I was young. or
any of these "three mermaids" alive I might have discovered the Secret

6

but the three. are Long since gone to kindred Spirits, the first to go was my reputed Grandmother. when I was about six years old. on this ocation I was the Chief mourner. (acording to Custom) very Strange indeed were the Circumstances. in Conection with the funeral &c but as thees belongs properly to the next number. of the "Translator" I shall Confine myself for the present to a strange discovery I did make while the three, were yet alive. Aunt Mortimer and Aunt Young. at the time I had no suspision thees two had any hand in the discovery but I shall give them the benifit of the doubt I entertain at present. it was the discovery of the "Stone Book" one of the most remarkable books ever writen by man. by man I do not mean one man for hundreds of men have writen this Book. but all of it is after the Same rule, or Maner. allthough there are three distinct Periods and each have their distinctive Carecter. again if I had had any idea about the Contents of this Book. at the time. I might have Coppied. Such parts that would be most interesting to the Reader and myself. what I actualy did Coppy. are not Lacking in intrest however — they shall appear in future numbers. unless I shall be fortunate enough to be able to take a facsimile of all of the "Book. in Stones" on one point. I am under a moral obligation. which I Canot break if I shall give the facsimile, it must be the whole of the Book. and that without any notes, or Coments whatever. but if I do comment or explain any part. or parts. I Canot give the facsimile. that is the Law, further I must Confine my Coments. Remarks, or explaination to the facts as shown by the Key. and not Strain the Meaning, to suit any Particular Idea, or theory, or refute Such. the facts and facts only, is the Law. in Conection with the Stone-book, was a Manuscript. Purporting to be a translation of a part of it. by Some one Styling himself <u>Reverend</u> — this is Called the Lirpa-Lauoph, and is in very old fasion English —

allthough of the Merit of the Translation, j do not entertaine very high apprecian, but it has been a valuable help to me to translate the Heiroglifhics. and the Songs of the Mermaids, to which j so offten in my zauth listend, have also been of greet benifit. but more than all was the Ceremonials. which j absserved at first, because j was taught to do so, and afterwards. because those in whome j had the higest faith. did so. after these were gane, and j was left alane to perfaum thees peculiar Ceremanics. j began to daubt their utility, and the facts which appear in Canection with them, Seemed at ane time Somhwat hipothetical, to me. but j never ance faild to abserve them nevertheless. and naw since the Cantents of thees Heiroglifhics, have given me a new Light. and a key to this wonderfull Stane-Book, it is a great Satisfaction to me naw to be able to Cantinue the observances of thees remarkable Ceremanies withaut ane break; and naw knawing the meanig therof, j can do so intilligently, and with a "Prand faith" and if need be j can laugh to Scarn the Saphisty of thare pretenders, and Supernaturalists. and Scientists so Called, who pretend to teach peaple phillosaphy, of the true Nature of which they actualy Knaw nathing at all, as far the three Mermaids, j cancat Say haw far their Knawlege reached, but j knaw as a fact, they were the Mediums of a remarkable mistery, j have repeatedly heard their Questians answerd fram "belaw the Sea"! when they performed the Ceremanies on the sacred Share of Zeman, &c it may be News to Many Readers, to be told that if any of them will take the trauble to Stand an "Sarn Badric" or Caer Gwyddno, which are in Cardigan Bay, or any such as was at ane time the Land of Zeman at a Certain time of the year, and at the Passage of a Certain Lunenay over the Sea that naw Cavers the Sacred home of the Ancient Gods (Neigals) between whaine and the Druids, there was an Ever lasting Cavenan they Shall withaut fail hear Samething they Shall never after forget. or daubt

Modern scientists teach, that the internal parts of the Earth is nothing but a mas of liquid fire! why? because they have discovered that the surface of the Earth is such a number of degrees of heat, — at a 100 feet below it is hoter by so much more, allways increasin the deeper we go. hence they say it is only a simple mathenetical problem to prove the fact!!! oh, untamed wisdom what has become over thee, thou art not naturaly born? a Natural born, would never decended so low as thou hast, think of it four thousand miles, thou hast been thare of cours, or els how canst thou prove that the Center of the Earth is not a solid mass of ice!!! we at least know that the Poles of the Earth are cold, while the torid zone is hot. has thou yet to learn that the Earth is a thing of Life. why dost thou o my friend, follow in the blundering path of the Spiritualist, he at Least May be excused, since he has no intiligent material to work on or at any rate he beliveth so. and of cours his belife is nonmaterialistie too, not so was it with the Meirnaids. however their faith was mat-erialistic enough, and their Heaven also Made of very solid Matter. nor did they Look for it away beond the stars and the Ethenal blue, but face nearer, and within the Earth itself,! and they belived that they were in Telegraphic Cammunication with it also!!. and they belived they heard the words of the gods themselfs !!! kind reader did you ever hear of such a benighted belife before. is it not Manstrous, if you had been on the stage of Life at that time and had a vote in the Matter, what would you have done with such unchristian philasophy. would you not have comited them to "Sheol" or very likly at that time this sheal was unknown, and to Place was called by Some vulgarer Name, (what could j say, More vulgar) well as you pleas, a little gramer is not much here nor thare, as long as you and me mean the same thing, by the same words, or signs. but lett me ask as a favour, that you shall take for granted my words as j shall explain them, and not attach meaning to them that j never intende them to bear.

In the year 1800 at a young Ladys school in the West of England three young Ladys, heretofore Strangers to each others, became fast friends, their names in full were Mary Mortimer de St John, Mary Temanmaur Young and Mary Morvrin Evans. The first was a native of the west of France (Brittany), the 2nd, of the west of England (Cornwal), and the third from the west coast of Wales. The curious part about them is that their names are nearly the same Literal meaning: John, Young and Evans all mean young, and the second name, Mortimer, sea of the house of Mer-Mercury

Teman Maur (Mar), house of Man~
Place of the sea, Morvain (Sea
of the hill~Maunt). and because
of this reference to the Sea, doubt~
less, they received the name of
MERMAIDS. When I was a boy
the three resided in Cornwal, and
once every year they (with others)
visited a famous stone circle and
a certain cave & relics, observing
some ceremonies, the object

and nature of which at
that time was unknown to me,
particularly the one on the sea~
shore, in which I allways appeard
as having the Chief Part to play.
I was taught to say a number
of verses

in a language unknown to me then, but which I have lately discovered what it was, or partially so, at least. Mary Morvrin Evans married one Captain Robarts, a native of Cornwal. The other two as far as I know, were never marid. The oldest son of Captain Robarts also became a Captain and part owner of the ship _____. I was taught, and believed, that he was my Father. But recently I have discovered that he had saved me when a baby not a month old from the shipwreck of his ship, on bord of which I had been since the 2nd or 3rd day after my birth ~ and he had

adopted me as his son, my own parents having been lost in the shipwreck, whoever they were. If I had only even suspected these particulars, when I was young, and any of these 'three mermaids' alive, I might have discovered the secret.

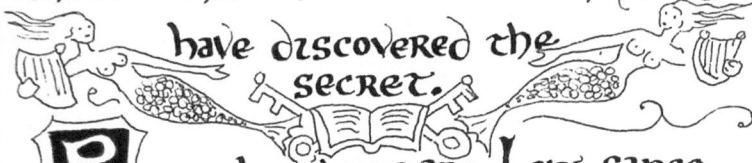

But the three are long since gone to kindred spirits. The first to go was my reputed grandmother, when I was about six years old. On this occasion I was the Chief mourner (according to Custom). Very strange indeed were the circumstances in connection with the funeral.

But as theese belongs properly to the next number of 'the Translator', I shall confine myself for the present to a strange discovery I did make while the two were yet alive... Aunt Mortimer ... and Aunt Young. At the time I had no suspicion theese two had any hand in the discovery but I shall give them the benefit of the doubt I entertain at present. It was the discovry of the 'STONE BOOK' one of the most remarcable books ever written by man. By man I do not mean one man, for hundreds of men have written this book, but all of it is after the same Rule, or maner. Although there are three distinct Periods and each have their distinctive character, again, if I had had any idea about the contents of this Book, at the time, I might have coppyed such parts that would be most interesting to the Reader and myself. What I actually did coppy are not lacking in interest, however ~ they shall appear in future numbers. Unless I shall be fortunate enough to be able to take a facsimile of all of the

'Book in stones' on one point, I am under a moral obligation, which I canot break, that if I shall give the facsimile, it must be the whole of the book, and that without any notes or comments whatever. But if I do comment or explain any part, or parts, I canot give the facsimile. That is the Law Further I must confine my comments, remarks, or explaination to the facts as shown by the Key, and not strain the meaning, to suit any particular idea, or theory, or repute such. The facts and facts only, is the Law.

In conection with the Stone book was a manuscript, purporting to be a translation of a part of it by some one styling himself Reverend '___,' This is called 'the LIRPA-LAUPH' and is in very old fasion English - Although of the merit of the translation I do not entertain very high oppinion, it has been a valuable help to me to translate the Heiroglyphics. And the songs of the MERMAIDS to which I so often in my youth listened, have also been of great benefit -

but more than all was the ceremonials which I observed at first, because I was taught to do so, and afterwards, because those in whom I had the highest faith did so. After these were gone, and I was left alone to perform thees peculiar cere monies, I began to doubt their utility, and the facts which appear in conection with them seemed at one time somewhat hipothetical to me. But I never once faild to observe them nevertheless. And now since the contents of thees Heiroglippics have given me a new light, and a key to this wonderful STONE-BOOK.

It is a great satisfaction to me now to be able to continue the observances of thees remarkable ceremonies without one break; and now knowing the meaning therof, I can do so intelligently and with a 'Proud faith', and if need be I can Laugh to scorn the Sophistry of those pretenders, supernaturalists, and scientists so called, who pretend to teach people phillosophy, of the true nature of which they know nothing at all.

As far as the three mermaids, I can'ot say how far their knowledge reached, but I know for a fact, they were mediums of a remarkable mistery; I have repeatedly heard their questions answered from 'Below the Sea' when they performed the ceremonies on the sacred shores of Teman, etc. It may be news to many readers to be told that if any of them will take the trouble to stand on 'SARN BADRIC' or CHER GWYDDNO which are in CARDIGAN BAY

OR any such as was at one time the Land of Teman, at a certain time of the year, and at the passage of a certain Lumenary over the sea that now covers the sacred home of the Ancient Gods (MERGALS), between whome and the Druids, there was an everlasting covenant, They shall without fail hear something they shall never after forget, or doubt. Modern scientists teach that the internal parts of the earth is nothing but a mass of liquid fire!

Why?

Because they have discovered that the surface of the earth is such a number of degrees of heat ~ at a 100 feet below it is hoter by so much more, allways increasing the deeper we go. Hence, they say it is only a simple mathematical problem to prove the fact

O unthmed wisdom

what has become over thee, thou art not naturally born? A natural born, would never decend so low as thou hast. Think of it. Four thousand miles.

Thou hast been there, of course, or else how canst thou prove that the center of the earth is not a solid mass of ICE [][][]

We, at least know that the Poles of the Earth are cold while the torrid zone is hot. Hast thou yet to learn that the Earth is a thing of Life [][][][?][][][]

Why dost thou, o my friend, follow in the blundering path of the Spiritualists? He, at least, may be excused, since he has no intelligent material to work on, or at any rate he believeth so.

Is it not monstrous? If you had been on the stage of Life at that time and had a vote in the mater, what would you have done with such unchristian phillosophy? Would you not have comited them to Sheol or very likely at that time this Sheol was unknown, and the Place was called by some vulgarer name, (what could I say: more vulgar?) Well as you pleas, a little gramer is not much here nor there, as long as you and me mean the same thing

And, of course, his belief is nonmaterialistic, too. Not so was it with the mermaids, however. Their faith was materialistic, enough, and their Heaven also made of very solid mater. Nor did they look for it away beond the stars and the Etheral blue, but far nearer, and within the Earth itself! And they believed that they were in Telegraphic Communication with it, also. And they believed they heard the words of the gods themselves. Kind reader, did you ever hear of such a benighted belief before?

by the same words, or signs. But let me ask as a favor that you shall take for granted my words as I shall explain them, and not attach meaning to them that I never intended them to bear.

Spelling

When the papers were illuminated we decided in keeping the integrity of the originals and did them exactly as they were written.. even with spelling mistakes. English was John Hughs' 2nd language after Welsh.

Listed below are those words that are Roberts distinctive style in spelling.

Three Mermaid

Grandmothers' House

In the Three Mermaids we read of how John Hugh as an infant in 1828 was in a shipwreck and his birth parents drowned. He was saved from the raging sea by Captain Roberts. He was raised and taught the ceremonies by three women,.. one was his grandmother and pictured below is her original home in Llaniestyn, North Wales. The lady of the house read the geneology John Hugh had written and said that his grandmother was a relative to her. Both her husband and her were both fascinated with the story and the writings of their ancestor.

Guides and Friends

Dale's "Inner Merlin" quest started at the Rainbow Rose Festival in California at the Pasedena Convention Center in 1979. He had previously lost
his hearing in his left ear and had decided to see a Dr. David Davies, a scholar as well as a healer. He was delayed in seeing him and went into a room where a lecture was taking place by Rose Gladden, a British healer, while speaking the lady went into a trance and an 'ancient being' channeled through her, and told Dale he would be involved in healing. Soon after this he saw Dr. David Davies and later had a strong intuitive feeling to study the Druids. Days later while visiting his mother, in Vancouver, found she had inherited these writings of John Hugh Roberts from Charles Steele, his grandson. Dale then went on a quest to understand both the manuscripts and himself. Dr. David Davies became one of his mentors along with Everid Helweg Larson-Young, who was one of the first lone white woman explorers in South America, visiting Easter Island, Galapagous and China in the 1930's and 40's. Two other friends were Bill and Patricia Meilan who travelled with him on one of his many trips to Wales and introduced him to many people there.

THE RAINBOW
ROSE FESTIVAL

Everid Helweg Larson-Young

Patricia and Bill Meilen

Mermaid Dream, Chair and Mermaid Cove

Dale's wife Della had a dream of a mermaid and felt upon waking realized that they had to do further research on the papers ... Dale had been talking about going to Wales, England, Ireland and Scotland. and his first trip of many was in the very early 80's , and since then has returned many time to Wales. Living in Birmingham, England for a year gave him the opportunity to further his research in Wales.
While there they went to Cornwall and met Sue Bladon who kindly opened her home to them. Relating the story of the "Three Mermaids" she was told of a story of a mermaid who fell in love with the choir master in the 1600's in Zennor, Cornwall and ended up sitting in the carved 'Mermaid Chair' in the local church. Sue Bladon and her friend Barbera Tremain took Della and Dale on a trip around to see many important stone circles. Barbera held the "Three Mermaids" papers and got a strong intuitive feeling of where to go. On the right is the cove where she felt some of the ceremonies took place.

Friends who helped us - thank you!

In our travels exploring and researching around the British Isles we made many friends who helped us there. Living in Birmingham, England for a year we were able to travel and research in Wales, Cornwall and Ireland.
Three of our friends who helped, John Baldwin, Elwyn Roberts (who drove us on a trip around Wales) and Marian Hall who we travelled with us to New Grange, Ireland, along with opening up their home to us in Birmingham. Thank you everyone!

John Hugh Roberts 1870-1917
This shows the family of John Hugh Roberts - his wife Anne, Sarah, Missi and grandchildren.   Also shown is his son Tomhu Huron Roberts who became a noted artist and at the bottom Charles Steele his grandson who was the first boy registered as being born in Vancouver -(1886). Charles passed the Druid writings to his friend Mary Bertrand .. Dale's mother.

The Roberts Heritage Foundation presents

Vancouver–The First Years 1884–1917
Record by John Hugh Roberts Sketches & Paintings by Tomhu (Tomtu) Huron Roberts

John Hugh Roberts

**Record Keeper/Writer –
In Vancouver from 1884 -1917**

John Hugh Roberts was a prolific writer who wrote detailed diaries for 60 years of the life of his family. In looking at the diaries we can discover a lot about Vancouver. Roberts and his wife Anne were together for 60 years and their family of two daughters and a son were very close.

The Robert's Women and Girls- Anne-1828- 1922, Winnie (1882), Mary Missi Roberts (Sippi) 1857- 1932, Flossy 1895-, Sarah Anne Erie Roberts (Sis) 1855-

From the John Hugh diaries we get a lot of insight into the every-day to day lives of the Robert's women/girls. Their daughter Sis (Sarah), who was widowed twice, lived in Winnipeg but visited Vancouver occasionally.

There is many references to John Hugh's wife Anne in his diaries, and their daughter Mississippi (Sipp) who lived in Vancouver, and her daughter Flossie. Both sisters travelled a fair amount back and forth to Winnipeg, Toronto and Vancouver.

Part 3
Turn of the Century Women

One of the first Artists Registered in Vancouver– Focusing on his Vancouver period from 1884 -1917

Early Canadian Artist - Tomtu Huron Roberts was one of the early pioneer artists in Canada who painted the natural beauty of Canada. Contrary to reports of him being born in Wales, we know from his father's diaries, he was born in 1859 in Collingwood and since he was born on the shore of Lake Huron was given the middle name Huron.

He entered the Real Estate and in 1908 opened a business on Pender Street West. He went to school at Mount Pleasant.
From John Hugh Roberts's diaries we read of many visits by his daughter Sippi and his grandson Charles Steele.

Charles Steele by Tomtu H. Roberts

CHARLES STEELE
PIONEER REALTO

LISTINGS WANTED

Charles Steele's life - focusing on the years 1886-1917

Part 4
Charles Steele 1886- 1970 The First Registered Male Child of Vancouver

Charles Steele was the son of Mississippi & William, nephew of Tomtu, and grandson of John Hugh & Anne Roberts. He was born on Alexander Street in 1886 and as there was no registration office in Vancouver they had the birth recorded in New Westminster - the first to take place.
He was suppose to be called "Vancouver" but his mother objected as felt it would be shortened to Van and would sound too Dutch.

His father worked for a while as a photographer and went in partnership with his brother in a photography company called Steele and Co. Ltd., in which Charles also apprenticed in 1904. Wonderful family portraits as well as records of Vancouver were taken. His father later worked at the Old Hasting Mill and then as locksmith in the old C.P.R. Roundhouse on False Creek. Because his father worked at the C.P.R, he got passes to travel, and

did so many times to Winnipeg and Toronto. John Hugh comments in his diary of 1904 "Charles F.H. Steele passed the examination for bookkeeper at Pitman College" - first boy born in Vancouver after the fire".

from Sketchbook Tomtu H. Roberts

John Hugh Roberts
Writer

Author - "Last Recorder of the Druids"
John Hugh Roberts was a Welshman who lived both in Toronto and Vancouver Canada from 1850 - 1917, with his wife & family of 2 daughters and a son. He worked first as a tailor, and then as a land developer, buying, developing and then selling the land. For sixty years he kept detailed journals of his life. They had a house at Quebec & 10th & later in Point Grey. In his final years he wrote the various stories and poems from his life and "The Stone Book of Knowledge". He indicates the information came from old stone tablets in Wales. Scholars have speculated these mysterious papers may of originated from the Akashic Records. He wrote these papers to be read by future generations and meant them to be published but they remained hidden away until 1979 and in 2014 - released to the public.

Dale Bertrand

Researcher, Producer and Adventurer

Dale is a lover of the mystical and magical in life. He has travelled extensively fulfilling his Druidical Quest for knowledge. Applying lessons he learned from his travels in other countries during the 70's and 80's he decided to follow his intuitions in decision making and very soon after this, synchronistical events started to happen which allowed an "Inner Merlin" Quest to flourish. Researching the Druid manuscripts and diaries by John Hugh Roberts, has taken him a dozen times to Wales, and also Ireland, Scotland, Cornwall and in following up on some of the more unusual leads to Peru, Guatemala, and Mexico. His inner journey and sharing the writings of a Druid at the turn of the century has resulted in the 'Druidical Quest' published in 2008. He has also produced various selected stories from John Hugh Robert's writings which have been illuminated by Leo Del Pasqua -- 'Three Mermaids', 'Gaelcerth of Halloween', 'Chief Festival of the Druids' and 'Nennius'. He is open to ideas for collaborations.

Leo Del Pasqua
Artist

Leo did all the wonderful illuminations of the Druidical Quest, and Illuminated Books. His art comes under many names such as Visionary or Conscious Art - he calls himself a Practicing Symbolist with a specific interest in contemporary Spiritual Art. He holds a Master's Degree in Theology from the University of Toronto. Examples of his artwork and poetry may be viewed at Urantia's "Brother Leo's corner" from Ottawa on line. Leo also has Ebays Veronicas Liturgical Art and is co-partner of a store which opens in the spring called "Getz Better in Old Killaloe" where some of his art is displayed.

Thanks!

Thanks to so many people for helping with this project over the thirty four years of development.
To John Hugh Roberts for his inspirational work.
Dr. David Davies for his integrity and motivation. Della for her motivation, perseverance and especially for her love. Everil Helweg Larson-Young & Dr. Henryk Binder for their wisdom and sense of adventure. Doug Atkins for his eagle eyes in finding the Stone Book of Knowledge.. Mary Bertrand for her love and instilling the love of "history". Jim Young for saving so many important books in the 40's and 50's from destruction. Leo Del Pasqua for his wonderful illuminations. Bill & Patricia Meilan for sharing these mysteries and for his poetry and both for their love of Wales. Stevanne for support. Cayo Evans for his love of Wales and his great Welsh hospitality. Shanti (John) Baldwin for his transcriptions and friendship. Dr. Jordan Paper for co-journeying to magical North Wales, etc. Elwyn Roberts and Marian Hall for sharing their home, and the adventure. Sue Bladon and Barbera Tremain for the Cornwall adventures. To all the Directors of the Roberts Heritage Foundation Mary Lynn Ogilvie, Edna Reti, Joanne Williams also Jules Atkins, Tom Williams and all the Williams family, Michael, Pat, Diane, David, Loosie, Howard, Alice, Virgil, Bruce & Mark and Wallace. To Glen, Brenda, Rob, Laura & kids, Warren, Murray, Golda, Chris, Flora, Holly, Norah and all of the Burford family including the late Desiree Burford. Harri for helping the vision, and to all family and friends Sorry if I have forgotten someone. Thank you all so much.